ALPHABET

Andrew S. Guthrie

Supported by

Hong Kong Arts Development Council fully supports freedom of artistic expression. The views and opinions expressed in this project do not represent the stand of the Council.

Alphabet consists of twenty-six poems concerning the vagaries of failure, the underrated opposite of success. But in this case, the context of failure necessarily includes the genre of contemporary poetry, that most disabused yet over-abundant mode of expression. Why would anyone choose to express themselves in a manner that automatically narrows the readership, even after dispensing with avant-garde ambitions? – Precisely because its condition might lend itself to the aimless, useless or extra-economic moments when success can be turned on its head. And though the poet might be prone to the audience's neglect, history itself is rife with countless examples of spectacular literary failures (as addressed in *Alphabet*), whether these traumas are eventually redeemed or forever lost. These examples include: misplaced manuscripts, writer's block, articulate illiterates, libraries that were burned to the ground, posthumous fame for the previously poverty-stricken, botched yet endlessly repeated translations, along with the obvious shortcomings of the dilettante, the over-inflated ego, and the perennial loser.

Andrew S. Guthrie was born in New York City, lived most of his life in Boston, Massachusetts USA and moved to Hong Kong in 2005. In Boston, he exhibited at the Boston Institute for Contemporary Art in 1996 and was awarded a Massachusetts Cultural Council Fellowship in Photography in 2003. His artist edition "Broken Records: 1960 -1969" has been collected by The Brooklyn Museum of Art and is available from Printed Matter in New York City. In Hong Kong he has exhibited at The Shanghai Street Artspace, Videotage, C&G Artpartment and most recently at 100ft.PARK. In 2012 he established www.likink.com, a Hong Kong based site for the distribution and production of artist book/editions. He has previously been published on the websites of Make Do Studios and Weaponizer and in the print magazine *Poetry is Dead*.

ALPHABET

Andrew S. Guthrie

Proverse Hong Kong

Alphabet
by Andrew S. Guthrie.
2nd pbk ed published in Hong Kong by Proverse Hong Kong, July 2015.
Copyright Proverse Hong Kong, July 2015.
ISBN: 978-988-8228-09-6
Printed by CreateSpace.

1st pub. in pbk in Hong Kong by Proverse Hong Kong, 9 April 2015.
Copyright © Proverse Hong Kong, 9 April 2015.
ISBN: 978-988-8227-22-8

1st ed distribution (Hong Kong and worldwide):
The Chinese University Press of Hong Kong,
Shatin, New Territories, Hong Kong SAR.
E-mail: cup-bus@cuhk.edu.hk; Web: www.chineseupress.com
Tel: [INT+852] 3943-9800; Fax: [INT+852] 2603-7355

1st ed distribution (United Kingdom):
Christine Penney, Stratford-upon-Avon, Warwickshire CV37 6DN,
England. E-mail: chrisp@proversepublishing.com

Distribution and other enquiries to:
Proverse Hong Kong, P.O. Box 259, Tung Chung Post Office,
Tung Chung, Lantau Island, NT, Hong Kong SAR, China.

E-mail: proverse@netvigator.com; Web: www.proversepublishing.com

The right of Andrew S. Guthrie to be identified as the author of this work
has been asserted by him
in accordance with the Copyright, Designs and Patents Act 1988.

Page design by Proverse Hong Kong.
Cover design by Andrew S. Guthrie.

All rights reserved.
No part of this publication may be reproduced, stored in a retrieval system, or transmitted, in any form or by any means, electronic, mechanical, photocopying, recording or otherwise, without the prior written permission of the publisher. The book is sold subject to the condition that it shall not, by way of trade or otherwise, be lent, re-sold, hired out or otherwise circulated without the publisher's prior written consent in any form of binding or cover other than that in which it is published and without a similar condition including this condition being imposed on the subsequent owner or purchaser. Please contact Proverse Hong Kong in writing, to request any and all permissions (including but not restricted to republishing, inclusion in anthologies, translation, reading, performance and use as set pieces in examinations and festivals).

British Library Cataloguing in Publication Data.
A catalogue record for this book is available
from the British Library.

Previous Publication Acknowledgements

The poem, 'Grammar School' has previously been published in, *Poetry is Dead: Inside Outside*, Issue 01, Volume 04, 2013, Vancouver, Canada.

Alphabet *by* Andrew S. Guthrie

Table of Contents

A: files	1
B: manuscript	3
C: rehashed manifesto	5
D: vanity press	7
E: consignment	8
F: notebook	10
G: anthology	12
H: entertainment	15
I: open mic	17
J: bookstore/book shelf	19
K: thought	21
L: syllables	24
M: pre-antiquities	29
N: unsorted	32
O: intermission	34
P: hallucination	37
Q: grammar school	39
R: well-known	43
S: quivering slice	44
T: zeus	47
U: dilettante	49
V: lost fonts	51
W: justified	58
X. x marks the spot	60
Y: your edit	63
Z: kill the poets	66
A review of *Alphabet* by Ching Yuet May	71
Advance Responses to *Alphabet* by Viki Holmes, John King, and Daniel Zomparelli	72

A. files

If you've been paying for storage space
for left-overs, hold-overs,
to-be-revised
refurbished
re-shod, soon-to-be-resold scenes,
what jewels are hidden there,
what brand of
charcoal?

If the curator is self-appointed
then how can the self-named archive
install
sheathes of bark,
animal skin scrolls,
shards of embossed mud
and the endless
electronic
cache?

Files
generations of flies. They burnt down
the library (Go to the temple and sacrifice
some paper).

And then we will start
over again
once again
among the curious flies
like we might be
(blank slates)

the first
technologists.

The poet's obscure
meritocracy.

B. manuscript

When I had submitted
my final manuscript
by way of a "cold call"
sent on the static
a hieroglyph
on the capsule's door
pulled apart
by forces beyond our recognition
they couldn't put it back together
again
anytime soon.
They built the structure
from whatever
was left. I needed a roof
over my head.

The second verse
was the same
meaning shot through
the electric canon
and into cyberspace. We could extrapolate
the context
and thus wrote about it (at length)
but basically
understood little.
The context exciting enough (for our purposes).

Someone found it
washed ashore
a soggy repurposed
carpet.
They began to write on the reverse.

C. rehashed manifesto

Where do we go
after we topped the horizon
and smelled our own
backside?

The columns are getting loose
and here and there
stragglers drop whole lines,
not marking a text
but trailing off.

We looped the globe
shattered the camera's perspective
and still haven't pictured
the other side.

We are still waiting
and use waiting like a voided banner,
a farce to match
the gaping hole.

There is a-too-well-known glory down yonder,
a down-on-your-heels reverse dimension,
an endless stretch of overcast days
making for a creative output
with the heady weight
of a shot.

The rehashed manifesto
is flying
its tattered flag, a tag line,
an incorrect citation
where nothing else will suffice.

D. vanity press

I tore open the envelope
and swallowed a vanity press. A bulk order, a
crumpled ball
before I entered the elevator.
I tried to forget about
the embossed title.

And when the doors opened, that crack between
solid and moving things,
the shaft that dropped, dead space,
and what was down there? Discards
plucked from mailboxes.
School notes. Receipts.

The dead air shaft
with its mulch pile
of spent notes
or worse,
windowless
unless the top is blown off. There is subject matter
down there
but hardly prose. There are marks, scratches
layers
of plaster, paint, smoke,
dust. A concrete block.
Maybe
a magazine.

E. consignment

You're as bitter as dusty bug-chewed pulp,
the progeny of worse-than-death lectures and petty
grammatical sleep deprivation!

Cast out your meagre book,
and your dragging alliterative syllables,
costumed like the manuscript
was still housed!

Go ahead and take your deluded field notes
strewn with dubious procrastinations;
the scene that you can't see so well!

Take it to the narrative holes and non-linear glitches,
you deep bright first person shoveler!

And if you could stand on that platform?
Pee in biography's tub?
You would only repeat yourself after your best seller sold,
let alone make the page count,
the tome inducing stupor that spells out your erratic spelling!

Get a day job and a hotel room
and bury yourself in the endless task of piling pages,
you blank pencil sharpener!

And when you receive another dent in your proverbial script,
no one asked you to take an interest in something that had no interest in you,
you drip coffee desk scratcher!

Stop demanding that anonymity be interested in your unlisted acid-burned file card
documenting tenuous proof of an under-the-ground shoebox text!

Take it back to the copy editor,
the office shredder,
the suicide note rejection door!
Shove it in the ever ready consignment sale
and go back to your leaky roof residency,
the directory
of the world wide land fill!

F. notebook

Up in the attic,
where things are catalogued with dust,
not properly sent
but ditched,
your next of kin is simply relegated to the narrative arc;
her grotesque trunks well-imagined
but thankfully stowed.
Embroidery,
becomes her first medium
until she holds the notebook close.
She is writing a letter to your Mom,
digressing within its formula,
something about
weak tea and wind across the linoleum,
cushioned wooden chairs
next to an electric hearth,
a shawl to cover
the notebook.

She began to write the novel,
furtively,
between insistent visitors.

A letter to Mom
(she writes Mom every other day)
from her redacted residency,
noting persistent solicitors, insistent visitors,
plot twisting creditors, interviews by staff and intern
soon to be released.
She is made unaccountably anxious
about her next jump (looming outside the window).
A diary, a dairy, ink spots, milk on the ledge,
an idea after lights-out
feverish
on her dark room's pillow.

Her ration of cigarettes gave out
but she continues, reusing tea bags
with milk preserved between winter
and the electric hearth.
Dear Mom,
this is not a gold mine where you dig for treasure
but a loft full of atmospheric residue
and vernacular manuscripts. This is a memory of me,
the unknown subject
of a second hand photograph.

G. anthology

He pencilled words
on a crumpled post-it note
on the top of a manhole cover
in an expensive school's
back lot,
those necessary
but well avoided spots
that maintain sand
between asphalt cracks. Beloved of weeds
this one had over done it,
over-grown and dried out,
salted with plastic bags. Nevertheless,
they saw you
trying to hide there, to get away with nothing.
That's why it looked so odd.

He mimicked contemplation
like he was
writing
something
down.
until the rickety structure gave out
(the note went in the wash).

It was like he was actually
falling over,
a rogue bum, the badly read white son
of the middle class
too fit for passer-bys to care
but disturbing enough
to shun

He walked by the anthology's address
over and over,
back and forth,
the address of the mimeographed
post-graduate sheet
in his pocket;
the ivy-covered facade complimenting
its limited run. The creeping vines
covering hand made glass,
casting cathedral light
on the diorama.

Typewriter manuals lay
on defunct mantelpieces.

Someone he used to know
or met once, someone he saw across the room
at the auditorium
saw him pacing
back and forth
through the ivy shaded wavy glass of odd
circumstance.

Eventually they disappear
but where do they go,
the types and kinds, individuals, unknowns, passing by
pacing back and forth
or falling over?
You never met them,
but you run into them
without map
or even percentages,
they come and go
with one foot suspended,
waiting to pick up
where they left off, waiting to collect the books they
lost
when their lease ran out
in the outer precincts
of a college town.

H. entertainment

It doesn't speak the language, or any language we know
or language as we know it. Its species and gender
are unknown. But it knows
speech or speaking, pre-historical clicks
and gestures. It invented
ritual
so it knows how to get in line.

It recognizes the alter, the stage, the symbolic phallus
that you cajole;
that they speak into. That they step up to
and begin. One by one
they emote on stage under dramatic torch light,
cigarette smoke
and heckling. A subterranean
temple.

After it is introduced
there is an interminable pause
and it still hasn't started,
or has it? More pauses,
a lunging towards the microphone. Wheezing
and some cockroach syntax, a bird call.
Nothing we could call poetry,
spoken word, or direct communication.
And the restive audience
begins to holler.

The creature is extremely shy
and/or traumatized
or is indicating
a collective trauma – torn from pure sensation
and subjected to vicarious entertainment. More long moments
where blank and roughly folded leaves
fall from its paws.
spittle inflected hisses
and the indefinable noises we make
when we collect our thoughts,
when we collect ourselves,
somewhere between
a laugh and a cry.

The master of ceremonies sweats
improvises thank you
and applause. The speaker makes
one last long curtain rendering holler
powerful enough to remember
after everyone else's literate star
has faded.

I. open mic

The kid hadn't spoken for days except for the
occasional purchase
or work. On the weekends he didn't say anything. For
hours
or even days. So when he stepped up to the
microphone,
it was by surprise,
a kind of surprise,
something he didn't quite expect
even though he had planned it. Planned it for days
or years. At work
it occasionally crossed his mind. He imagined the pose
out of place and out of context, like the frame of a film
in a magazine. He kept magazines under his bed.
He erratically wrote poems
low numbered
in a lined notebook
in a backpack.
He was going to read one of those. On a Tuesday
night.

This is how his poem went, after he had paced
back and forth
in front of the coffee house.
This is the actual poem, a facsimile from the original copy,
found in a lapsed storage space.
The poem he read, or stumbled upon,
in a cafe that sold coffee but which required a scene.
A stage,

something to get people to drink coffee
on a Tuesday night. The scene opens up
on scuffed wooden tables, wi-fi
a scruffy staff and the occasional professional.
This is the poem:

"I finally received something in the mail
like the writer in Truman Capote's Breakfast at
Tiffany's
unpaid advice that went something like this:
'While this poem has interesting flashes of
simultaneity,
as if we are present
during its inscription,
at this time we would be more interested in your
progress
than the enclosed submission, Sincerely,
Denise Levertov.
Ladies and gentlemen, that's the truth, just as I stand
here before you
right now, in your presence, speaking only for you, and
you alone.
Who else
would this be for?"

J. bookstore/bookshelf

The ordinary cramped used bookstore
a low rent walk-up
or inherited basement
containing canyons
of sculptured stacks
unpainted pine shelves
squeezing corridors
filled with lost titles,
day old discards,
ancient lists, improvised recipes,
unmanned conspiracies,
travel-less pictures,
blank pages,
thin brittle abbreviations,
heavy weight amateurs,
low and high
publishers
and
over-stocked
designer brands.

This curio shop
in the well-known narrative city of perpetual war,
in the city where America
was first bombed;
pre-owned items that offer
an inkling
of another time's
relative affluence.

Excess carried over
and hand picked from the trash.

It was in this very brick building
that Edgar Allen Poe dawdled,
among these same shelves
where your shadow
now selects
a recently remaindered title.

These same pulp board and laminated shelves
offer you a title
by an old friend,
one of your old school chums.
You recognize the face but not the name.
The name but not the face.
A local lost budget publisher
for local poetry
with its timeless
ISBN number.

K. thought

Someone got there
before me
had the same thought
more or less
before I did.

I once thought something like that.

It was suggested
by a lost-to-history writer (a playwright with no story)
later forgotten, a phrase
that turned up
in the later works.
Someone else ran it down,
but was later
mistaken.

It was the detail that was forgotten
but there was nothing less in the world (as opposed to
space).
The clouds still dispersed
or dissolved,
their wispy traces
vanishing up yonder. What did it say?

It might have been significant.
Signifying something
of note. A lost connection
between two wires, two planets, an intuitive leap
from element
to atom
until
I lost track
of its shape.

All my files crashed,
disconnected.
The library offline,
but it should still be in my head
(cranium)
somewhere (but the wire may be bent
out of shape).

The themes, if not the weight
will be the same; the general outline
obvious.
Easy to distinguish,
because it struck a chord
all the right notes
that I forgot
to note.

I am repeating myself.

The inside of my head
organization
appears on the screen
like a dishevelled
larder
more like
a bloody pulp, leaky,
waiting a billion years
for the latest
news.

Did I leave something out?

L. syllables

One mouth is doing
all the talking.
on and on, and on, on,
no longer syllables
but an unbroken line.
A continuous tone.
The subject is stuck
on one subject. A refrain.
And swaying to it.
The speaker requires your attention
anyone,
an audience
of one.
Ignore
those patrons
at the bar. They think
they're better than me.
The tongue continues wagging
on this very bar stool,
broadcast on cable TV
(at 2AM),
in a neighbourhood library
(doors open at 9).
The resume continues
reading itself
underlining
the smudged ink-jet,
coming across
in week old tweed,

chest out,
elbow on the bar,
in a tobacco smudged shirt.
We're putting together
an archive
in this kid's basement.
The work under
a tarp.
The humming will continue,
drowning and drowning out,
dabbling in the old masters.
Those others, the enemies
over there, on the other side of the bar,
they're already published.
Who wants that?
Who wants that kind
of success?
The muscled jaw and dark grey matter
under a precious spotlight,
a promotional lamp from Budweiser.
The monologue could easily win
but abstains. Obviously.
We missed the deadline.
Let me tell you, let me say,
if the eyes looked closely,
held things tightly
like a mouth
and ignored the other ears,
then the fingers worked perfectly.
Only I could do that.
And this body won't do anything

without a buyer.
Where are . . . the
the party invitations?
When will this looped dream rid itself
of nagging rivalry?
In the cellar
where we all
began, and now reduced
to a chair,
a better location
for the ordinary costumer,
the common man,
those people get it,
those other people
don't get it.
I'm ignoring the museum.
The drone is pitching
almost automated,
aware of its rhythm, its cadence
its command of space; yet penetrated
with second thoughts,
reverse perspectives,
delirious heaves. The spotlight
no longer a glow
but sweating. Dew on the lip,
the responding drool.
I could easily serve the full menu,
seriously. The zines
want me back.
The larynx glides
unaware of a master, anyone who pulls

the chords. The song
too short or
too long?
The performer is asked
to repeat the chorus.
I am going to repeat that
when the publisher
finds me. It's being considered
but I'm quite busy.
And then I had to go into
advertising,
a substitute teacher,
an art handler;
during breaks I wrote
my unpublished notes.
The song that keeps repeating
in my head.
This cycle
will make me famous.
The audience of one or two
inside the maelstrom stays buoyant
by shifting attention
from the trumpet's horn
to its pock marks,
puts down the phone
without hanging up,
randomly interjecting,
"ah hunh".
I was the one
who made the call, I quoted
myself, and yet

the grant was denied, over and over
I quoted myself,
when someone
was tugging
at my sleeve,
I told them,
"vote for me". Get off the stage.
Is there any chance
you can lend me
a couple of dollars?
Finally it's winding down
like all our clocks,
its irregular pulse
exhibiting a lack of maintenance
while maintaining
its idiosyncrasy.
Can the audience muster an army?
That's what I asked myself
the last time I was here.
I'll be talking to you
later.

M. pre-antiquities

You the casual reader
outside the consequences
when
nudity, exposed
awkwardly raw, appears on your path,
disturbing your equilibrium,
shocking your average.
The mess tips a shelf,
rips a page.
It's the poet
who got one poem published.

It took awhile,
a lifetime
in the black hole
that mightily devours time.
The poet made a vow:
publish one,
publish only one poem.
So it had better take time.

The poet
who got one poem published
tried so hard
to fail, putting off
what you could do today,
tearing whole manuscripts
to pieces.

But writing is only half
unless you, the casual reader,
come across it
in a cave.
You know how difficult time is
going by
when the outcome is nowhere
in sight.

The nude, utterly unclothed
not-one-shoe figure
rearranged the message
and made a career
out of one short piece.
Totally nude
on your Sunday morning sidewalk.

When the poem
was finally completed
the poet deleted
all the other files, shredded the drafts,
scrubbed the blackboard clean, stripped
and placed the well-folded clothes
on a dishevelled desk.

At the entrance
to the cave,
the black hole's orifice,
you can see the entire oeuvre
outlined

scratched
in geological time. And before running by manicured lawns
the nude poet
recited
the last deletions:

"I know for sure
that the world
as we know it
will end
on the following date . . . "

Lines dropped,
deemed irrelevant
to the flow, to the general
structure,
excised
from the singular product,
finally accepted
by the Journal of Poetic Pre-Antiquities
of the Greco-Roman
Extension School,
Suburban Campus,
Phoenix, Arizona
Volume 5, Issue 2.

What's easier to remember
are the words of the arresting officer,
"Technically, no statutes were violated."

N. unsorted

Fondness for a dump, for those drafty floorboards
with a view on four lanes of heavy traffic.

An enigmatic nostalgia for the days of languishing, for stolen groceries,
for time afforded by being late to dead end jobs; we cleaned squid in a basement,
we gagged on fractioned tips.

A longing for what we couldn't wait to leave behind,
when sometimes we had to return to what we left behind
to falsely relinquish our meagre resources –
we ate leftovers from our parents' freezer.

Sweetness for an industrial squat, huge and cheap but sitting on a rocky foundation
with mismatched doors;
a former death trap with a sweeping view on a gold mine's parking lot.

The light-hearted memory of deathly fevers in frozen rooms made of discarded windows,
illnesses that coincided with the fast sound of rubber tyres on looping highways.

A lopsided grin for wheat paste smeared on chicken wire,
for vandalized text books, for spray painted walls,

for coffee brewed through a T-shirt.
A strange revision of hard times, turning the dirt under
our fingernails
into onanistic rebellion – a simpler time,
an easier depression,
a time of symptoms with short attention spans.

The regretful present for the bitter past when we
volunteered for beans,
for envious obscurity, for tawdry co-mingling and
communal clothing,
for sullied dreamscapes; we were even too young
for body odour.

We will never capture that sound again, those careless
lyrics that took less time
than a publisher's verbal contract;
we drank what was handy
and settled the tab with borrowed notes;
an impromptu shrine
to unsorted influences.

O. intermission

Now that we are half way through
the epic, let's take a break and assess
where the intermission should land.

After this break
there will be long sequences (around three to five hours),
so we should shift in our seats
and cough.

Let's just make sure
if we decide to come back to it
some other time
that we mark where we left off, and not let it drift
like a page
upon the waters.
So much has gone down the drain.

Part two (more or less)

In this interim
some of us were only able to recognize
a period.
The page went off the screen
and we took a break
before the stanza
was over.

(Somewhere in the theatre
the sound of snoring)

Has anyone guessed what this is all about
(now that we are
half way through
the interminable mythic passages
rendered in a botched translation)?
How difficult it is to read
something you're not used to! A scenario
that is dedicated to failure
and its brilliant, yet obtuse strategy
of testing our limits, of revelling in rejection;
its tedious freedom
for spelling out
its uselessness; its use of empty space,
of presumed intermissions,
masquerading as a grandly pathetic
alternate
lyric!

Dear reader
(because we are used to being addressed that way)
we will not go away despite your blank screen
(it was Mallarmé who discovered the page)
despite the lapsed modernity that poets used to exalt
(the future is still endless)
despite the rote mind of the browser
auto-filling your search engine

(anything can be poetry).

We will begin again soon.

P. hallucination

This movement was established to change the meaning
of poetry
but failed
to come to a conclusion. It was at a time when the
letter took over
what was left of the lyric, shifting the inference
from keeping the line going
to changing its direction. Nothing changed
but stories.

The head of this movement
had a rotten personality, sincere, rigorous, charismatic,
willing to cut your throat
over sentence structure. The boss expelled
deviants, though his movement
abused grammar.

Poetry had already ploughed this furrow, airing
allusion,
illusion, analogy and hallucination;
poetry was already on the wing, in the wheel,
on watery eyes
and within
inflated oratory. It had set an example
that this movement took hold of,
wringing out
programmatic
skits.

This movement failed to change
anything
except the way
this poem is written. Abrupt shifts, dislocated
angles. Bizarre adjectives.
This rotten leader is our patron saint
though he burns in the section of hell
reserved for those
who believe poetry
can parallel
power.

All through history, we idlers aimlessly jot notes
while representative men
versify anecdotes. Such are the strictures
of canonical movements
and text-book
manifestos.

Q. grammar school

These distinctive markings were first noticed
in the downtown area,
directly adjacent
to the Massachusetts State Mental Health Outpatient
Clinic
which is nearby the historic
yet unverified location
of Bronson Alcott's experimental
grammar school
(which was in existence from 1834 to 1837).

From there, the individual or individuals
who made these markings,
were able to extend their range
throughout the downtown area
all the way to the terminus of the MBTA Transit
System, and finally, as far as we can tell,
concluding with a few stray markings somewhere
around the location
of the colonial era Native American Praying Village
in Natick.

By markings, we mean writings,
words written on walls, lamp posts, utility and post
boxes
probably made with an ordinary magic marker
usually black, but sometimes blue, in block letters
that tend to curve downwards,
especially noticeable in the longer texts,

those which achieved the highest density
in the now obliterated area of Scollay Square,
an area known for ribald entertainment and tattoo
parlours up to
and including the late 1950s.

The usual subject matter for these markings
was the history and/or grievances this individual (or
these individuals) accumulated
in respect to the mental health providers that they, he
or she, encountered
within an unspecified time period
that may have lasted, indeed, a lifetime.
One marking that references actual medical
professions
or institutions
was noted near the former Beacon Hill residence
of the poet John Weiners (who died in 2002).

The lines of these markings are broken up and stacked
in stereotypical poetic form, and in some cases,
are separated into stanzas.
Besides these formal qualities, the language itself leans
towards the implied
rather than the directly stated,
and at times can elicit double meanings,
and ambiguous
conclusions.

There is one documented instance of this writer,
who we do not know whether to assign

the pronoun
they, he, or she,
alluding to two female poets:
Anne Bradstreet and Phillis Wheatly.
These references fit into the general pattern of a
delusional and paranoid
frame of mind, as these two figures are at once referred
to as patients
and doctors, as the unwitting subjects
of psychiatric drug trials
and/or fake identities
who practice medicine without license.

In continuance of a clinical diagnosis that vacillates
between lucidity
and chaos, many markings make references to a
conspiracy against the author
that subjects him or her
to an all-encompassing publishing ban, or otherwise,
appropriates and edits
his or her
original material
to suit the status-quo of medical literature.
The author also notes
his or her marginality, frequently referring to the
author
as: "outsider".

While our uncertainty as to whether these markings
were made by more than one person
might seem at odds with such a distinctive style,

it has been observed
that occasionally
the markings have been photographed, photo-copied
and then pasted to various surfaces.
In these cases, which are much rarer
than those done by magic marker,
a type-written note is added
on top of the photo-copy
citing various works of literary criticism, albeit in a
disorganized and scattershot fashion.

One of these cites Richard Burgin's interview
with Jorge Luis Borges,
though the quote is altered
to make it appear that psychiatry and its abuses,
the cost of health care,
and the architecture of mental institutions
should become the major focus of contemporary
literature.

At the start of our study it had appeared that the
distribution of these markings
had reached an apex, and indeed it appears that,
due to natural erosion
and/or state or corporate sponsored maintenance,
they are fast disappearing.
This would also indicate
that the person or persons involved
have ceased or at least curtailed their activity. There is
no way for us to know
whether this is a temporary or permanent situation.

R. well-known

The advice/hint/information you gave me
though I have forgotten your name
changed everything.

I second-handed your idea
though it rolled off your tongue.

I lost the URL
after countless links.

Your name
a poem
with broken links.

You have disappeared
with a trace.

Your presence
a thought
that comes to me
in between
every well known taste.

You know who you are.

S. quivering slice

The documentation video
focuses on your dry lips
and shaky hands, the quivering slice
of paper,
the way you scratched your balding head
and trailed off
at the end
of a line.
One can hear the reverberations
of a space left empty,
but
there is no shot
of its emptiness.
You don't see the blank
faces,
those few members
of the anonymous
audience.

After your suicide
the critics recast the shape
of the podium.
Though you are far from heaven,
the video has been
enhanced
to include a halo.
No contemporary
commentator
mentions the apparent size

of the long gone
low numbered
and dedicated
audience,
because now . . .
you are posthumous.

Now
you are a captive
of posterity.
You captivate those
on the flipside
of failure. Your hand-to-mouth
an academic thesis.
Can they have lent you
a dollar?

What the record doesn't show
is the camera's pathetic tri-pod,
the folding chairs stolen from a bingo parlor,
the implied sound of wind,
the drafty architecture of desperate venues,
and one of the lonely
audience members
with a pet pigeon
on her shoulder.

You have been archived
a complete set of volumes,
facsimiles of original drafts, in ironic counterpoint
to drafty architecture.
Your original and meagre audience
dispersed.
Pet pigeons banned
from the climate controlled
acid-free
archive.

She was the one who went
to every performance,
reading, staged reading,
open mic, in-house salon,
poetry slam,
gallery opening, open studio,
opening night, sermon,
speech, lecture,
round table discussion,
dress rehersal and
street corner premiere.

But she didn't write anything
down.

T. zeus

Paste the proofs on the wind
and let the template
blow
in your ears.

The wind doesn't make a sound
unless it hits
something.

One sunny day
the apocalypse arrived
on a greeting card.

I read about it
in a book
that I found on the beach.

What is this thing for?
It doesn't grow on trees.

The tree was thrown into fire
or mashed into pulp.

All the machines will break apart,
even the ones Zeus made.

I can't guarantee anything.

This book will come out sometime
in the near or far future,
after more pressing matters, other priorities,
after the busy season.

Sheets of paper,
thin and tasty slivers of mashed tree
are dancing
up and down the shore.

Their delicate humour forecasts
the end of it all
and the ominous wind
is laughing too hard.

U. dilettante

I can see there's a lot of money in poetry,
poetry books and poetry stores,
lucky professionals
and eager dilettantes. Academics
and poet laureates,
street corner bards
and iconic ferries.

There are handsome boys and girls
with no more
than pen and paper
in hand.

Let me give you an example.
I'll take all of today's headlines
and write a speech.
cut-up from free newspapers,
because no one's reading
the pay-fors. I'll write a speech
built from online headlines,
because that's where all
the traffic goes.
I'll submit it online;
a peerless
redundancy.

I was mistaken about not liking poetry
as I was mistaken about not liking
The Ramones.
I backed into sculpture
staring too intently
at prose.

I went into a poetry store of historical renown,
a store the size
of an historical marker;
the one without security cameras,
a room the size of two or three
interconnected closets,
and asked for the latest hit record.

I asked,
"If I have only one book of poetry,
if I only have room in my record collection
for one book of poetry,
if I only have one book of poetry
lying around for when I get around
to reading poetry, what would you recommend?"

V. lost fonts

The blank white scroll returned his ass-aching stare,
the raw squandered surface
hung-over by his flushed
opus.
That blank page
that used to be much
more
friendly,
now an insistent, inanimate, smooth or crumpled
nudge. Not even a thing, a sculpture
or a functional object; just an unused, tossed
surface.

A blank.

(11:30 am, July 19, 1979,
222 W. 23rd St., Manhattan,
The Hotel Delmore: I check in, lay out my works
and lie down. I have told no one
of my whereabouts, or what I intend to do. An overcast
day
full of hot air and muffled sounds. I put pens, pencils,
typewriter, paper
on the desk of empty drawers
and lie down.)

(In my slumber I hear
the muffled sound of Disco
coming from
the dashboard speakers
of a passing car.)

The ritual objects have been relieved
of their magic.
A vessel is set nearby
naming itself fuel
but without movement; an unreliable watered-down
primer.
The next plateau only a view
on lost fonts,
lost contacts,
overdue contracts.

(Constant snippets of Disco
wafting from streets, cars, bars, radios.
Saturday Night Fever finally made it from #1
to the gutter.
When I am entering the frayed yet genteel hotel
I see the whole double album
discarded in the gutter
broken.

I am attempting the well-tested but unproven
formula. I will avoid the dance floor until
my masterpiece is finished. I must be willing
to revive the discarded, and discard
my usual
moves.)

At one time
he put the star gaze into the cracked binding,
he was the deep reader of moldy folds;
taking long looks
into the crevice
where two priceless pages
met.
He went out of the library,
into a scholarship,
backed into a scholar
and received full tenure.

But the next big thing
kept piling up
and slipping away
despite and because of
the flash; the pre-order
outweighing the sale. The enticing concept
teasing unrealized
steps.

There must be more than this
or at least
more of this.

(I could use that kind of
segue; the repetitive chorus, simple but open,
generously interpretive. I can comprehend the possible blending
of lyrical content
as well as
nascent beats. But all that I can manage so far
is this hesitant diary. They expect more
of me.)

They were losing track of him;
the dreams listed on last year's roster.
He is going head to head
with the final chapter, pacing the hotel room's
rug,
all the sounds muffled. He is all alone
now
with the era's background noise.

Muffled melodies coming through double paned
windows,
plaster board,
and sun-blocking drapes. Toilets flushing
on another floor.

(I hear Native New Yorker wafting from a Bodega, a
song that is upbeat yet melancholic,

underground yet commercial,
sweet yet cynical,
obvious yet obscure.
It glares at me on street corners,
standing sticky outside stores
just a few blocks south
after midnight
where I have gone
in my rumpled suit and tie
to retrieve a package that may inspire or
kill time.)

(I am being mistaken for one of the neighbourhood's
left-behinds
trying to weave in and out
without standing out,
desperately trying to weave my own ideas into
rigorous hermetic combinations
that emphasize
metrical formulas. It's driving me crazy
and I'm likely to be shot
if I wander too far.)

He hoped for the best
when the shadows rolled him
on the Lower East Side.
He had the advantage of
money in the bank
a suit and tie
and a clean face. But what was he doing down there
when the Pentecostal superintendent

kicked him off the stoop,
when the whores
propped him up
and pocketed
his notebook
sensing its heft and potential,
tucking it in the crevice
between Botanica candles? The whores who could never locate
the secondary market, the literary agent, the library collection.
The pilfered notebook
gathered wax
and fused
to the shelf.

(Because I saw it spinning on the record player
under an orange
and bare
25 watt light bulb
in that unholy sanctuary
where I was brought back to life,
I stopped at a 24 hour outlet
on East 23rd
and bought The Salsoul Orchestra 12" Disco single. I have nothing
to play it on
and I misplaced my notebook
so I am writing this
on the record jacket. July 20, 1979,
6:30 am. I will display this record jacket journal

when I am finished. I will take whatever is left
and make the most of it;
this unfortunate incident has given me
a trope.
The problem is
that it will require
that most despised of forms:
free verse.)

No matter what form
you received it in, no matter what frequency you
received
on the dance floor,
or when you read those exact words,
or knelt next to a record player,
or walked under the stars
on the dodgy margins of a foreign neighbourhood –
that exact moment is passing
though you are unable
to let it go.

(The rhythm builds
and then releases the break.

These
are
the
breaks.)

W. justified

So many itchy writers
lost or hidden
inside the noggin.

Lost or buried texts destroyed by close relatives
or the hired help.

Lost holidays dedicated
to unemployment insurance
and anxious space; the largesse
to write.

Unsympathetic relatives
housing the older brother's / younger nephew's
psychotic ambition to write
a mystery.

Justified existence
though our breath is unimpeded. Double edged
ambition, the residue of egos. Thoughts
that have been organized, notated
and then left without
a second thought.

They say that a writer
writes, but what if they write
and then stop writing,
never finish,
or write once
and not twice?

I kept going to the well
looking down in the hole
and seeing the reflection;
but seeing is not the same
as describing.

I wrote a whole book
about that.

X. x marks the spot

Nothin' has to happen
for there to be our story.
Words
comin' out of our mouths
tellin' things;
the sound of happenins', so to speak;
the times we went somewhere
and settled down;
and those that, along the way,
fell off.

Those speeches are like water
in a river,
unreported twigs
rushin' by
while that big old log,
(some tree that got named)
backin' it up.

None of us never knew no cyphers
though we surely spoke,
made noise,
wrangled over events; memories
in and out of order; phrases remembered
and then reversed.
We could speak, that's for sure,
so the letter writer
wrote it down.

A half penny per-word.

But what did you want to say (what was worth the
tellin')?
There was the story
and then there was space: that horse just standin' still
like time was froze,
(slow as stars in the sky).

Some of us did know the words
to a few songs, a whole baleful of lives
and livin'
packed into a few tunes, a few choruses,
a handful of lyrics (floatin' on the ether). That there
was surely
us (me and him).

On the other side of the figurin'
was the hard and fast notary,
pointin' to a dotted line
tellin' me to sign
with my one letter –
"X marks the spot",
I took his word
for what it was worth, and put the pay
in the purse. We all knew
the count,
if not the type. That small type
above my X.

That's all for now, Ma.
Your daughter standin' on the corner of this here far-flung town,
under the awning
and on the planks
next to this here
letter writer, his scratchin'
and markin' like a fever, a map of germs,
like the grip from another planet.

Y. your edit

1.
Someone with revelation (in his own tongue) dragged
suppressed flesh from a hole
and recounted the adventure, the quest, the question
and answer
to the dropped jaws
of neophytes.

Direct contact had been made,
accounted for and then recounted
on the page (many years after the event).

The scripture was dropped back in the hole, hidden
from scoffers, rearranged by rot,
rewritten from memory, rediscovered and reapplied.

Why do you wander so, a singular mind in the
sprawling cityscape, when your father's library
is like a vineyard, when his word bundle might staunch
the aimless unknown?

2.
The priest said, "I know what you mean . . . ", looking
into the deep archive
of the shrine
where the hole once stood. The scribes worked around
the edges; the occasional mystic

retrieving commentary
after a nap in the sun.

This then . . . was a different school of thought, making
the ecstatic utterance
less flexible, till the translators lost track of the word
for
"mirage".

It's out there in the desert where strange things happen,
the deathly silence
dislocates
wind from psalm. Scorching vapour might be
deified neglect
or a trial topped
by quenching floods.

3.
He said unto them,
"A rain will fall . . .", but he wasn't talking about drips
or drops, but the space between evasive
signals.
He is tinkering with the machine, a tinkering
mechanic;
A seer
with a few good words. A theory doctor;
a demagogue disclaiming
the answer (just one among many).

What gives him the right
to say the words are not his alone,
but everyone's,
the ambiguous vocabulary that suffers
from imprecise grammar,
an impenetrable code
rendered in cuneiform,
taken from a mountain top conference
where he swears he saw
a face?

Behold, even the stone falls apart
yet my stance is petrified. My stanza without author
(though archaeologists
keep scratching). We are the word, the record,
the book
straight from the original source; straight from a
faceless mouth
to a selective ear.

4.
All these are your edits,
the temple hacks that funnel speculation into a
definitive version, an artificial stream
straight to the palace garden.

And I say unto you
don't alter the alteration.

Z. kill the poets

Kill the poets
because they are only at war with themselves,
meeting in small columns,
hardly enough
to fill a category,
keeping an epic or a couplet
in the front of their minds
on the company clock,
or in someone else's
trench.

Kill them
because they refuse to say exactly
what it means
exactly
saying it actually means
many things
at once.

Even facing a firing squad
they dispense with pledging
recognizing
the inherent limits
of the idiom.

They serve no purpose
serving no time
but the time in between jobs,

losing track of the economy
writing in prisons
or on a pension; willing to rest in broad tombs
or a meagre hole.

This is why
they are so dangerous.
They stand apart
willing to lend a hand
but keeping their own thoughts
intact,
diagramming a kind of thinking
that could never be followed
while still locating
a rocky path.

Kill off the poets
those who are stubborn enough to accept all the
variations;
from strict meter
to free verse;
those willing to move from New Orleans
to New York City
and back again.
They are only dogmatic
in the infernal saloon,
only patriotic
in the god-forsaken
out door
school.

Their genre needs to be expunged.
The world can do without this epistolary immorality,
this language without practical use.
The poets must be wiped-out
to make way
for better paying jobs.

A review of *Alphabet* by Andrew Simpson Guthrie

This volume cleverly juggles with the twenty-six counters of the English alphabet to conjure up poetry. The reader hears the voice of an aspiring poet persona who persists in the creation of this literary form despite all odds. He, she, or we or they (identities shift and merge in the poems) must devise and revise, write and rewrite, as well as retrieve from memory, revisit past scenes of folly or glory, and woefully get rejected. A glance at the first few titles, all humbly in lower case letters, will reveal a poet's career through the veneer of irony, a trajetory from "files" to "manuscripts," from "rehashed manifesto" to "vanity press." Then poetry has to be promoted like any commercial product as "entertainment," in "open mic," or displayed in /on the "bookstore / book shelf." Finally though, words still get mangled in "your edit," and the injunction to "kill the poets" concludes the volume.

    The pervasive irony of the volume demands from the reader a constant alertness to the layers of meaning. Thus the reading experience is enriched, and highly rewarding to one who cares about the place of poetry and the role of the poet in the modern-day world. The reader is not challenged too harshly though, for the poems are often humorous, the effect enhanced at times by a sleight of hand with rhymes. Free verse is used throughout the volume. It has a casual and improvisatory quality, as it can quickly modulate to playful rhymes, wax ostentatiously prosaic as in "grammar school," or become wistful as in "zeus."

    This volume of poetry revels in antics of the mind that also spin off to wanderings in the maze of a city, thus opening up the self-reflexivity of the poems to the sights and sounds of an urban centre. In the poem, "grammar school," downtown Boston serves as the backdrop of a mad run of strange markings. New

York is the setting for another poem, "lost fonts," where a novice poet locks himself up in a hotel room to write up his masterpiece while city noises and voices keep on wafting into the hotel room and into the poetry. The volume merits recognition from still another city, Hong Kong, for the readers there, as readers elsewhere, may like to enjoy deciphering the strange markings that have strayed across borders.
—**Ching Yuet May**

Advance Responses to *Alphabet*

Andrew S. Guthrie is a poet's poet, and his collection *Alphabet* views life through the lens of the written world, from cuneiform, to typewriters, to the links of a URL. Guthrie's poems are situated in a world familiar to any jobbing poet: bookstores and open mic sessions, publishers and audiences. In twenty-six inter-textual and literarily aware poems, pausing for a moment to draw breath in the "intermission" of the poem denoting the letter O, Guthrie explores the impermanence and the irresistibility of the written word: a topic that both troubles and delights him. Everything relates back to the word, and is made sense of through the word, a loved one's name becomes "a poem//with broken links", and despite the frustrations and shortcomings of a written life, Guthrie's collection celebrates the poet's need to write as a scenario dedicated to brilliant failure. These poems portray writing as a cave, ventured into by the naked poet. If we wish, we can divest ourselves of our own preconceptions, and join his exploration.
—**Viki Holmes**, author of *miss moon's class*, and co-editor of the international women's poetry anthology *Not a Muse*.

Andrew S. Guthrie's *Alphabet* is a breathtaking meditation on iteration from the fringes of what might already be the fringes of literate culture (poetry), a doomsday journey of steaming technologies that has been failing for millennia. There is a metaphysical grittiness and vibrant wordplay to these twenty-six poems about the actualities of poetics and history that makes *Alphabet* a page-turner; that creates a space for poetry outside of the normal channels for the reception of verse, a space that is why we read poetry in the first place.—**John King** (director of the *Drunken Odyssey* literary podcast)

In *Alphabet*, Guthrie weaves and shifts through letters, papers, books, language and manages twenty-six well-crafted, varied takes on the culture of writing and the author. Writing a letter, reading a poem at a cafe, nesting poems within poems, *Alphabet* reminds us of what it is like to both drown and float in the spaces language and literature create.—**Daniel Zomparelli** (editor of the print magazine *Poetry Is Dead*)

WRITE TO US!

We are interested to read **your** comments on
Andrew S. Guthrie's *Alphabet*.
Write to our email address, proverse@netvigator.com,
giving us a few sentences which you are willing for us
to publish, describing your response to this book.
If your comments are chosen to be included
in our E-Newsletter or website,
we will select another title published by Proverse
and send you a complimentary copy.
Please include your name, email address and mailing
address when you write to us, and state whether or not
we may cut or edit your comments for publication.
We will use your initials to attribute your comments.

ABOUT PROVERSE HONG KONG

Proverse Hong Kong (PVHK) is based in Hong Kong with long-term and expanding regional and international connections.

Proverse has published novels, novellas, non-fiction (including autobiography, biography, history, memoirs, sport, travel narratives, fictionalized autobiography), single-author poetry and short-story collections, children's, teens / young adult and academic books. Other interests include diaries, and academic works in the humanities, social sciences, cultural studies, linguistics and education. Some Proverse books have accompanying audio texts. Some are translated into Chinese.

Proverse welcomes authors who have a story to tell, wisdom, perceptions or information to convey, a person they want to memorialize, a neglect they want to remedy, a record they want to correct, a strong interest that they want to share, skills they want to teach, and who consciously seek to make a contribution to society in an informative, interesting and well-written way. Proverse works with texts by non-native-speaker writers of English as well as by native English-speaking writers.

The name, "Proverse", combines the words "prose" and "verse" and is pronounced accordingly.

THE INTERNATIONAL PROVERSE PRIZE

The Proverse Prize, an annual international competition for an unpublished single-author book-length work of fiction, non-fiction, or poetry, was established in January 2008. It is open to all who are at least eighteen on the date they sign the entry form and without restriction of nationality, residence or citizenship.

The objectives of the prize are: to encourage excellence and / or excellence and usefulness in publishable written work in the English Language, which can, in varying degrees, "delight and instruct". Entries are invited from anywhere in the world.

The Prize
1) Publication by Proverse Hong Kong, with
2) Cash prize of HKD10,000 (HKD7.80 = approx. US$1.00)

Extent of the Manuscript: within the range of what is usual for the genre of the work submitted. However, it is advisable that novellas be in the range 35,000 to 50,000 words); other fiction (e.g. novels, short-story collections) and non-fiction (e.g. autobiographies, biographies, diaries, letters, memoirs, essay collections, etc.) should be in the range, 80,000 to 110,000 words. Poetry collections should be in the range, 8,000 to 30,000 words. Other word-counts and mixed-genre submissions are not ruled out.

KEY DATES FOR THE PROVERSE PRIZE IN ANY YEAR
(subject to confirmation and/or change)

Receipt of Entry Fees/ Forms begins	No later than 14 April
Deadline for receipt of Entry Fees/ Entry Forms	31 May
Receipt of entered manuscripts begins	1 May
Deadline for receipt of entered manuscripts	30 June
Long-list announced	July-September of the year of entry
Short-list announced	October-December of the year of entry
Winner(s) announced	March to November of the year that follows the year of entry
Winning book(s) published	Within the period, beginning in November of the year that follows the year of entry
Cash award made	At the same time as publication of the winning work(s)

More information, updated from time to time, is available on the Proverse Hong Kong website: <www.proversepublishing.com>.

The free Proverse E-Newsletter includes ongoing information about the Proverse Prize. To be put on the free E-Newsletter mailing-list, please send your request to: <info@proversepublishing.com>.

POETRY PUBLISHED BY PROVERSE

Those who enjoy "Alphabet" may also enjoy the following poetry collections / poetic works also published by Proverse.

Astra and Sebastian, by Lawrence Illsley. 2011.

Chasing Light, by Patricia Glinton Meicholas. 2013.

China Suite and other Poems, by Gillian Bickley. 2009.

For the Record and other Poems of Hong Kong, by Gillian Bickley. 2003.

Heart to Heart: Poems, by Patty Ho. 2010.

Home, Away, Elsewhere, by Vaughan Rapatahana. 2011.

Immortelle and Bhandaaraa Poems, by Lelawattee Manoo-Rahming. 2011.

In Vitro, by Laura Solomon. 2nd ed. 2013.

Lifelines, by Shahilla Shariff. 2011.

Moving House and other Poems from Hong Kong, by Gillian Bickley. 2005.

Of Symbols Misused, by Mary-Jane Newton. 2011.

Painting the Borrowed House: Poems, by Kate Rogers. 2008.

Perceptions, by Gillian Bickley. 2012.

Rain on the Pacific Coast, by Elbert Siu Ping Lee. 2013.

refrain, by Jason S Polley. 2010.

Shadow Play, by James Norcliffe. 2012.

Shadows in Deferment, by Birgit Bunzel Linder. 2013.

Sightings: a collection of poetry, with an essay, 'communicating poems', by Gillian Bickley. 2007.

Smoked Pearl: Poems of Hong Kong and Beyond, by Akin Jeje (Akinsola Olufemi Jeje). 2010.

Unlocking, by Mary-Jane Newton. 2013.

Wonder, Lust & Itchy Feet, by Sally Dellow. 2011.

OTHER GENRES

We also publish in other genres, including fiction (novels, short story collections and novellas), autobiography, biography, children's illustrated books, educational books, Hong Kong educational and legal history, memoirs, poetry, teenage / young adult books, and travel. Other genres may be added.

FIND OUT MORE ABOUT OUR AUTHORS AND BOOKS

Visit our website
<http://www.proversepublishing.com>

Visit our distributor's website
<www.chineseupress.com>

Follow us on Twitter
Follow news and conversation:
<twitter.com/Proversebooks>
OR
Copy and paste the following to your browser window and follow the instructions:
https://twitter.com/#!/ProverseBooks

Request our E-Newsletter
Send your request to info@proversepublishing.com.

Availability
Most books are available in Hong Kong and world-wide from our Hong Kong based Distributor,
The Chinese University Press of Hong Kong,
The Chinese University of Hong Kong, Shatin, NT,
Hong Kong SAR, China.
Email: cup-bus@cuhk.edu.hk
Website: <www.chineseupress.com>.

All titles are available from Proverse Hong Kong and the Proverse Hong Kong UK-based Distributor.

We have stock-holding retailers in Hong Kong, Singapore (Select Books), Canada (Elizabeth Campbell Books), Andorra (Llibreria La Puça, La Llibreria). Orders can be made from bookshops in the UK and elsewhere.

Ebooks
Most of our titles are available also as Ebooks.

www.ingramcontent.com/pod-product-compliance
Lightning Source LLC
Chambersburg PA
CBHW051133160426
43195CB00014B/2459